THIS JOURNAL BELONGS TO

_____

Connecting with Your Inner Child

The purpose of this journal is to help you understand your emotions and how they influence your patterns and behaviours. To shine a gentle light on wounds of the past and make loving, healing changes in your life. Let Benny Blue support you to see yourself as a whole being rather than a fragmented self.

There is a little bit of Benny in all of us. He is a perfect guide, especially during tough times. He reminds us of the value of curiosity and the willingness to take chances and grow through mistakes. Let Benny take you by the hand and lead you into the heart of Benny Burrow, where your inner child awaits.

Use this journal to meet the need we all have to be heard, and to express what you think and feel without censorship. Self-expression is healing. This journal can be a safe space to share your heart's deepest desires or concerns — a place to connect with your inner child and show up as the adult presence they yearn for.

I am my inner self, and my inner self is me.
When I connect with my inner self, I stay true to me.

*I quiet my mind to hear the song of my heart.
The cauldron of my soul is refilled and replenished with love.*

I am worthy of admiration and respect. I love myself exactly as I am.

I am strong, fierce, free and capable of overcoming any challenge I see.

Let It Flow!

Brainstorming, writing or dictating thoughts and ideas can be helpful when attempting to streamline a fragmented mental process. Sometimes the mind likes to fire off too many things at once.

Writing ideas down gets them out of your head and on paper. It creates mental space and clarity. Journalling is an opportunity to slow down, ground and organise your commitments, free of entangled thoughts.

Set a timer for five minutes.

Before you start the timer, create the intention that you will write continuously for the full five minutes. Give yourself absolute permission to write anything at all without questioning or censoring yourself. (This may sound challenging, but try to approach the process with playful curiosity rather than expectation.)

When you are ready, start the timer and begin.

You might like to try this exercise every day for a week or longer. It's amazing what regular, free expression can reveal!

Remember — play and have fun!

*I trust that my pace,
progress and capacity
are enough.*

I enjoy the process of
EXPANDING
*in a healthy,
loving way.*

When I treat myself to life, I am treated well by life.

I am safe and supported in times of vulnerability. Having the courage to accept help when needed expands my potential for fun and new experiences.

*I am patient as I till the fields of success and splendour.
I plant my seeds, and joy sprouts within me.*

*Slowing my thoughts and becoming present help me rise with
strength, ready to face life with openness and love.*

I am courageous enough to express my wishes and open enough to accept them. My past does not determine my future. My thoughts, words and actions are aligned with the Universe. I choose to pursue my dreams.

When I remain grounded, I can weather anything.
I am open to the blessings of the storm.

I am the leader of my life. By following my intuition and trusting what's right, I am directed towards truth.

I embrace my emotions and allow them to guide me back to balance.

Create a Bubble of Ease

Before you engage in family events or conversations you feel some resistance around, practise this simple meditation:

Close your eyes and bring your attention to your base chakra (located at the bottom of your spine, close to your tailbone). This chakra supports your connection to your family or circle. Inhale deeply. As you exhale, visualise a ball of ruby light expanding beautifully and brightly, creating a bubble around you. Let this light act as an anchor to ground and centre you whenever feelings of unease arise. Visualise this ruby bubble anytime you are in need.

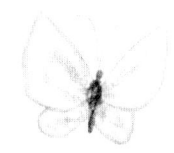

*I open to love
as I am opened by love.
I am safe with my*
BELOVED.

*I am free
when I let go of all
I am expected to be.
All I must be is
who I truly am.*

*Expressing myself with joy nourishes my soul and lifts my energy.
It is safe to let go and have fun.*

*All that I need will come to me. I let go of what no longer serves me
and travel lightly through life.*

*When I let go and have fun, I am more receptive to insights and inspiration.
My creative juices flow freely and easily.*

It feels wonderful to reward myself.
I am worthy and deserving of reward.

I am a radiant soul, gifted beyond measure. I shine my light in the service of others and don my cape with pride. I am superhuman.

I am patient with myself as I learn new skills.
I feel energised and relaxed during the creation process.

It is safe for me to be seen. I have all the resources I need to create the life I deserve.

*I draw upon the universal energies to flow with life.
I am calm and connected to all that is.
I exist in a state of perpetual balance and bliss.*

A Chat with Yourself

Given all that you've discovered about yourself since childhood, if you could have a conversation with your younger self:

How would you show up for yourself as a parent or guardian? In what way would you approach yourself? What qualities could you express to ensure your younger self feels safe, connected and comfortable to open up?

What questions would you ask? What would you be curious to know about your younger self?

What advice or guidance would you give to your younger self? What do you feel would have been helpful to know in order to navigate your challenges with confidence?

I absorb and retain information easily. I am open to ideas that feel good and right and gently reject those that don't. I love learning!

*I am the creator of my reality. I am worthy of abundance.
I receive good fortune with gratitude and love.*

I am a manifestation of pure love and light.
I bring peace to the world by taking time to simply be.

*I place myself in the hands of the Universe and overflow
with the energy of creation. I am enough.*

I make the best of every situation.
I see mistakes as opportunities to learn and grow with a smile.

*I have all the time I need to rest and replenish.
I am whole and healed with loving kindness and care.*

*With patience and trust in the process,
I transform into all that I desire to become.*

*Like the natural rhythm of the seasons,
I flow into change with ease and grace.
I am one with life.*

Questions to Contemplate

Some of us may have been parentified at a young age, meaning we felt we had to take care of our parent/s, rather than the other way around. We might also have felt mollycoddled, dismissed, unseen, controlled, over-protected, shamed or dropped, and the list goes on. I know we might be treading very close to some deeply emotional memories here — you may be feeling exposed and vulnerable. Rest assured, today is about the here and now.

We don't have to open old wounds in order to move forward. That can be an option with a trained therapist. However, today is about being present. You are encouraged to use the questions below to gain insights into your past that can improve your current and future life. By becoming more conscious, we develop the awareness and tools to support us when we find ourselves in a fight-or-flight reaction. We can learn to pause, breathe and—with gentle curiosity—ask our inner child helpful questions, like:

- ♥ Is this even your own fear, or are you reacting to a conditioned belief?
- ♥ Are you reacting to the actual scenario that is playing out, or is it something deeper? (E.g often when we express anger, we are actually feeling scared, etc.)
- ♥ How can you help me understand you better?
- ♥ How do you need me to be with you right now?
- ♥ What are you afraid will happen?
- ♥ What do you actually want for yourself at this moment?
- ♥ Are you responding to the part of you that we might call the inner critic?

Take time to pause after any or all of these questions and surrender any expectation of answers. Simply free-flow or check in with your inner child. They may simply need your company and acceptance of them as they are. Being present with your inner child can be just as impactful—and sometimes more helpful—than expecting any answers.

We can learn to be present and hold space for all that's within us — to become the parent or guardian that our inner parts need. By developing this ability, we can transform our internal environment from fragmented to unified and whole.

I am grateful for the blessing of my unique gifts.
I am open to receiving the Universe's gifts and am blessed to receive them.

*When I open to others, others open to me. When I am my true self,
I attract those who are true to me. I am worthy of belonging.*

I draw upon the inspiration of people I admire and seek to inspire others.

I polish the treasure of curiosity within me. I am delighted to discover my deepest desires and draw upon these gifts whenever I need them.

*I have faith in the stars, so I have faith in myself.
The Universe leads me into greater knowing.*

I love and accept all of me. I am perfect as I am.

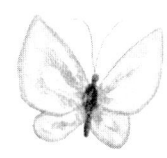

My feet are firm and planted.
My body is supple and strong.

My heart is one with
UNIVERSAL LOVE.

I may bend,
but I will never break.

I am open to receiving. Taking care of myself energises my body, mind and soul and expands my capacity to care for others.

*I lovingly listen to my body and give myself
permission to rest fully and completely.
I am grateful for all my body does for me and appreciate
when it lets me know it's time to rest.*

I eat my fill from the feast of the Universe. Endless abundance is available to me.

As I celebrate the daring of my soul, my joy brings joy to the world.

*As I greet myself in the mirror each day, I fall in love all over again.
I am part of the beauty I see all around me.*

*I am a unique soul with much to give to the world.
My bright colours and bold patterns make me beautiful.
I am precious beyond measure.
I am ready to be seen.*

*I am deeply thankful for everything I have.
The Universe blesses me with all that I need to give to others.*